THE SOFT BLARE

River City Publishing
1719 Mulberry St.
Montgomery, AL 36106

First Edition—2003
Printed in the United States of America
Designed by Lissa Monroe
1 3 5 7 9 10 8 6 4 2
Library of Congress Cataloging-in-Publication Data

Norwood, Nick, [DATE]
The soft blare : poems / by Nick Norwood.-- 1st ed.
p. cm. -- (The River City poetry series)
ISBN 1-57966-048-7
I. Title. II. Series.
PS3614.O783S64 2003
811'.6--dc22

2003017035

The Soft Blare

Poems by
Nick Norwood

The River City Poetry Series
RIVER CITY PUBLISHING
Montgomery, Alabama

for leslee

See how the absent moon waits in a glade
Of your dark self . . .

—Stevens
Blanche McCarthy

Contents

A Note on Nick Norwood's
The Soft Blare
Richard Howard

In his insidiously organized first book—it starts from an ominous prospect: *Tomorrow we'll be consumed by the work of a different master,* and concludes with an equally ominous retrospect: *Remember to mark your place in the story*—this new poet finds any number of formal devices and diversions by which to mark his inveterate theme, one (stately and compact) avouchment of which might well be Isaiah's *All flesh is grass.*

Severe enough, yet prophetic wisdom makes certain allowances; after all, if the grass is cast into the furnace and consumed, it must first come forth as the growing body of this death, and that is where Norwood seizes our attention and indeed our affection, for he is startlingly (because so naturally) incarnant. Nothing forced about this poet's Panic allure: W*here there was only the dim starlight, the night, the grass,* Norwood writes about a woman's vision of Erdgeist, *and it occurred to her she might be in love with him.* So it is not only natural but requisite that the work begins (as Virgil does, and Pope) with pastorals, so many convinced (and convincing!) icons of the earthly paradise:

> *We feel the pasture is perfect*
> *When all the vegetation is one.*
> *Let's call it lucerne, a pale olive*
> *Knee-high, each lithe stem*
> *An elegant drunk with wind-raked hair.*

Though even here in this first decade of poems, there is the declaration of underlying purpose: when we attain the pasture, paradise is merely death: *Come wait here for the snow,* Norwood beckons us, and it is only in the second decade that we shall learn the proper tone of voice in which to couch that invitation.

For these are poems of the actual embrace, the human entanglement with bodies, with art, and with history. How vulnerable the accents here, how modest the occasions, yet how memorable:

> *. . . A certain kind of silly rubbish*
> *has always helped me—deep down we are all*
> *face to face with a certain solemnity—we can guess*
> *that much—so I shall be silly till you want me*
> *to be sad, and then you shall have all the sadness*
> *that is in me . . . whether I see you or not.*

The sorrow of these clinches, as I like to call them, applies even more emphatically in the next group (only five, not the rule of ten here, for these poems in many voices are of a length), which concerns, with enhanced comical effects, the ludicrous loves and wars of Ludwig II as seen from outside— his architect, his gardener, his celebrated contemporaries. Except for Carl Jay Buchanan's set of utterances on Jack the Ripper, these Ludwig-lays are the best modern poems I know about the crueler follies of the nineteenth century.

Then on to the final decade of poems, which articulate Norwood's consent to see the grass withered and lost (though bled away in the "soft blare" of moonlight: that the poet takes his book's title from this phenomenon serves fair warning) in his direst poems, "For the Drowned," "Dichotomies," and "The Novel of Grisly Details."

Lest I sound a little too drastic in my sketch of this poet's enterprise as I read it, I must not fail to commend his wonderful mastery of the strictly lyric mode, so rare among his contemporaries. Norwood's poems in this register can actually be sung, indeed they seem to have the music in them already. And it is in the last, chiefly tragic group of ten poems that his intensest success in this kind of verse is to be found, to be heard, the final stanza of "Bluebonnets" properly articulating his lovely gift:

> *Sing for me*
> *Tumultuous field*
> *Your own trembling*
> *Arpeggios . . .*
>
> *O sing, sing*
> *Be my voice*
> *Rising, turning*
> *In yellow air.*

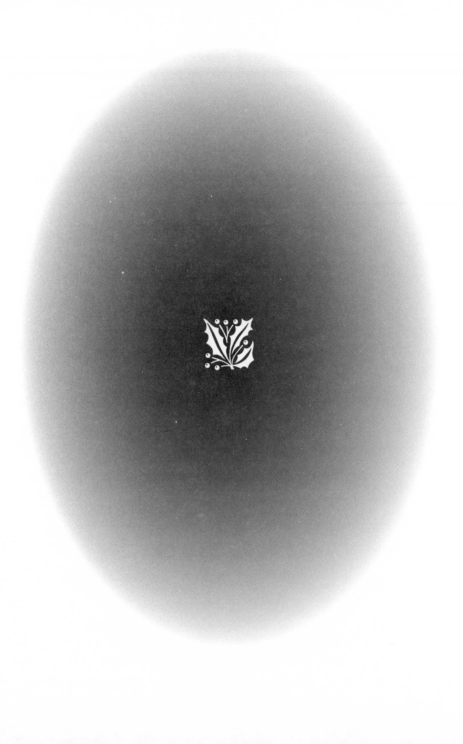

The Garden

Now that it is in your hands, this book, this page,
This entanglement of vines, notice how it struggles

Into the white space of air. Yes, it's too bad
It couldn't be more beautiful, resorts to the showiest

Of ornaments and can't produce a rose, a lily, a bearded iris,
Can't form a foxglove or forge a gladiola. We pity

Its attempts to imitate the mum. *Ah yes.* And so,
Forced to make do with a cold artificial light,

It spends its days dreaming of the sun,
Its nights aching that it cannot live without the moon

And does. A blanket of fog hovers above planted rows,
Deepens the mystery of their blooms in a plot it can only

Pretend. These are its failures, all it grows.

I

Song

Pastures are silly and the grass is dying.
Moreover, last Thursday, when she was with Jane
At the racquetball center, I stood in the bedroom,
My face just inches from the picture window
Overlooking the terrace, leaf-strewn and sad.
The house, settling, ticked like a cooling oven
And I thought of summer: raked meadows, sun.

Death of limb and must of earth. Trees
At the roadside, on the sides of hills,
Raise their arms in panic and end up
Like naked heathens caught in the act.
But this, too, doesn't print well, won't come off:
Too dark for a halftone. Ink smears and details
Are subsumed in a wash of gray and cloudy weather.

Meanwhile, in the valley, the hay is cocked,
The bells are ringing, cowbells and church bells,
The bells on her feet. I hear them as she jogs,
Attached to the shoestrings of her running shoes.
Past the barn, along the fence, in nylon
Shorts that seem to be made of the finest silk,
The definition in her calves apparent

As galoshes. She wore flowers in her hair
The night of the party, like a girl
From Greek myth or someplace in the country.

We proposed toasts to her, all of us,
Before we wandered off alone to this very room.
Our lovemaking—heated, passionate, etc—
Was followed by wind moaning through cracks

In the window frame and even after she
Spooned up to me, lay her head on my chest,
I imagined myself out there in the buffeted field,
Unclothed, braced against the heavy gusts.
A nettle, blown from its stalk, caught in my hair,
Dirt in my eyes. Haycocks began to fall apart,
Their flesh drifting off like . . . like loose hay in strong wind.

O part and parcel of this romantic pastiche!
Something you'd see on cable on Sunday afternoon
When other stations are broadcasting football.
O musical score weighted with gloomy strings. Tight shots
And close-ups and lots of underpaid extras as disinterested
Passersby. O past-your-prime actors, settling for life
On the small screen: I offer my material.

I'm here, in the bedroom, wailing a dirge,
While trees, mere skeletons of their former selves,
Click their highest branches. Her hair tails out behind
As she's running away. Her breath, in humid puffs,
Rises like dialogue bubbles in a comic strip and I'm
Reading the lines: cloudy, dense fog and a chance of showers.
Pastures are silly and the grass is dying.

Grandiflora

We read here, in The Great Book of the Golden One,
How we can only regain our human shape by eating roses.
Fair enough. And nevermind that under the microscope

They appear as nothing more than beasts of beauty.
Let's go into the garden, where it's cool now, the smell
Of peat less oppressive, and the mulch just rich enough

To remind us of pines moaning through windstorms.
Once there, with The Lion-Headed clenched in our fist,
The wind dying down, we'll let the rest of the story slip

Through our fingers. We've heard it all before:
The sun, the rain and the watering can, some chemist's
Reaction to a florid stimulus. The fragrance is just

Another way of saying *parfum*. We'd better save ourselves
For what is real, for something we can believe in.
Tomorrow we'll be consumed by the work of a different master.

The Unified Field

We feel the pasture is perfect
When all the vegetation is one.
Let's call it lucerne, a pale olive
Knee-high, each lithe stem
An elegant drunk with wind-raked hair.
That line of stubby hardwoods along the fence
Is nothing more than a frame, the single elm
Just off-center only there for perspective.
Otherwise it's all field no one has corrupted
With walking, no cow with grazing.
What is it, then, that we love so much
If not the sense of being extended
An invitation? Come, it says, live here
Forever. Mow, if you must, and watch it regrow.
Keep an eye out for the interloping weed.
Commit yourself to this little corner
Of the world and know at least that somewhere
You were able to satisfy your longing
For fulfillment. Come wait here for the snow.

Driving at Dusk in Open Country

The railroad right-of-way was furred with tawny grass,
And she thought, Look, there he is, lounging beside the tracks.
It's the miraculous beast who appears in my dreams.

She thought it better to look away. But in the end
She couldn't resist, glanced again. Still there. Stretched out
Like So-and-So reclining on his couch, eating figs. And

It occurred to her that she might be in love with him.
She began looking ahead to the arc lamps under which
His coat glowed golden in cones of light, imagined the feel,

The sleek suppleness, of his arms and legs, the dark
Strangeness of his torso. She knew it was just the dream,
But she pulled over anyway, between distant poles,

Where there was only the dim starlight, the night, the grass.

On Living by the Sea

Wind crashes through the trees
Like surf, surges, roaring in the limbs,
Its ebb a splattered inrush
Like retreating waves in the leaves.

Out here, far from any coastline,
These swells sound the vastness
Of an afternoon many-faceted
As storm chop. They part our hair,

Belly our clothes. We sit
In arid silence and watch the rollers.
Sublunary, ageless, immense:
The spirit if not the scent,

The spray, the body itself.

Roadside

And then there we were. Imagine our surprise,
Seeing ourselves up ahead, sitting in the skeletal shade
Of a bare catalpa tree by the side of the road.
We looked sad, hangdog, our heads slung
Between our shoulders, hands on our knees.

We seemed to be waiting for someone, or perhaps
Just waiting for something to happen. And
Something did: we glimpsed ourselves approaching
And watched halfheartedly, only following
With our eyes. We waved, but we didn't

Wave back. And then the long shadow
Of the limousine passed over our faces. The rush
Of wind we made scattered dead leaves
And paper trash, lifted them into the air,
Before letting them settle again at our feet.

We were almost out of sight when we noticed
The birds—crows, grackles—flying in
By ones and twos to roost in the upper limbs.
They, too, appeared to be waiting for something,
But, for the life of us, we couldn't say what.

After Midnight in the Mountains

A light lunar dusting of frost is on the tent,
And it's warm, beside you, in this sleeping bag
Made for two, but—isn't this always the way—
The coffee you brewed so deftly over the fire
Is reasserting itself, driving me into the whiter world
To tip-toe from stone to stone. And after a minute
I call to you, try to wake you up, whispering at first,
Then louder, more insistent: there's no moon, come look.
And from the great cacophony of stars I hear how passions
May conflict. Quick, come see before the moon rises
And bleeds it all away in its soft blare, in its great
Now and forever of slow-gliding stillness, telling us,
Emphatically, that all there is to love is stony light.

Hill-Climbing

It's all right with me that the promontory rises up
Like the face of a god. Hills stand still. Stay put.
We'll make it. And look: a swarm of bees
Working a bed of wild irises, untended, all alone
Up here in this middle of nowhere that is the lost
Everywhere of the world. See how they fail so sweetly
To notice us. There's no other garden for them.

There, now we're here. And see: the sky, waiting
For us all this time. A gathering of stones
Big as hogs lounging like cows in a summer pasture.
The view: nothing but other hills, the earth
Wasting its way over the horizon in all directions.
That lone pine across the ravine casting its dollop
Of shade. And us, here, wishing we were there.

Pleasures of the Highway

A silver barn in a summer pasture:
The shine of corrugated steel
And sheen of crenelating grass
Are one and the same. The sky

Itself seems backed by something glass,
As if, say, a mirror were behind
The air, reflecting the sun, retracing
The way we move. Our forward motion:

Concession to uniformity.
If we could stop, we'd sprawl in the field.
The wind and the traffic would whisk
Their single way. They'd sing in our hair,

Which would fly like the grass, our eyes
Rayed with sparks like sunlight in chrome.

In Trees

Late winter, the flesh-scrapped skeleton
Of a beast buried to the waist

In a vacant lot, its arms ending in gnarled fingers
Knuckled with pecans

That didn't fall. Squirrels raid the corpse
Like rats, crunch the bones,

Tooth and claw. It's the only sound to break
The silence, assuage the blistering

Distance between this field in morning
And the terrifying engine

Of the sun. All afternoon, a lone tree stands
Upright against the weight

Of the sky, weight of the cold, holding
Its own, and waiting.

In the evening, starlings come to roost
Hump-shouldered

In its upper limbs, their sheer numbers
Calling forth the darkness,

Casting shadow, a brooding Hitchcockian gloom.
Strollers choose other routes.

(The streetlight's burned out and no one's come
To fix it.) The wind

Dies and the air sets up like cement.
The flock,

Settling into a solemn quiet, assumes
The shape and color of night.

There's nothing left now but the branches'
Coming entanglements

With the moon, their life, and our own,
In stars.

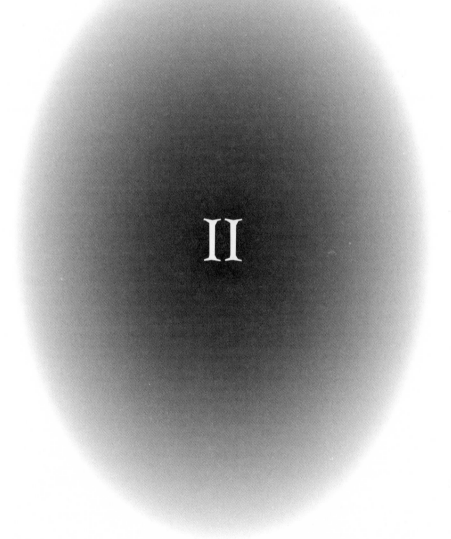

II

A Made-for-TV Movie

He begins to notice how all his single friends have dogs
And wear expensive running shoes, how their conversations run
To deep metaphysical questions that didn't exist before 1983.
Chance encounters in coffee shops near the university.
Driving home alone in the late afternoon. Solicitous phone calls.

As always, it's the transitions he's lost track of. That was then,
This is now. Like a goof, he wonders what will happen next.
But it won't be news. Even the dog owners know this. They,
More than anyone, experience anxiety as a force of nature. He's heard
Their loopy descriptions of it, like cosmological treatises on string theory.

Inevitably, the dog has been saved from a dark fate at the animal shelter,
There have been broadly comical evenings of obedience training
At the local park, doggie surgery to correct a hip, cataracts, gum disease.
On a whim, he buys a ticket north to catch a genuine autumn, and
On a fluke, there's a cabin vacant at creekside. But it rains all weekend,

And the promise of color turns dull and soggy, like, he realizes,
The whole idea was to begin with. He leaves early to return the rental
And decides to stop at a roadhouse with barn-brown siding. A shapely
Beer glass on a tiny round table that wobbles, the sound of eight ball,
Country-Western music, and highway traffic. He'd vomit, but it would seem so

Theatrical, here, in this place, far from any life he ever wanted. Who
Would believe such a story? He happens to look down at his shoes, which
Seem shyly to comfort one another, his sturdy footwear, leather to leather.
Outside the window, the rain has stopped, the eaves keep dripping,
The glossy-wet macadam reflects the sad, tawdry lights of this little dive.

Pillbox

There, on the top step of the rollaway,
The tarmac gleaming, wind-whipped, under a cold sun,
And the crush against the cyclone fence
In gloves and overcoats, waving, she thinks,
I ought to blow them a kiss. But she turns instead

To Sunday afternoons. The beach, the sand stretching out
Like a blinding smile, and the waves pressing up,
Loving it, and loving it, and loving it to death.
She adjusts her sunglasses—dark, impenetrable—
Searches and finds the limousine, then takes a first

Tentative step. Another. It wouldn't do
To stumble now, with only cameras there to catch her,
Only wool and bone to break her fall. She holds tight
To the handrail. But even then she feels a sudden sinking.
Or is it a lifting up? The roar of the engines overwhelms

The people's screaming. They are all motion and
No sound, and they are smiling so. And then—
Who can say why?—some three steps down, she lives
Her life from start to finish. It flickers before her
Like a home movie, slightly overexposed. And it is good

For the most part, as lives go, but still sad in the end.
Not tragic in any splashy way, just leaking slowly out,
Like the last inch of water after a bath. An old woman
In pumps worn past their season, making her way,
Awkwardly, down a long corridor, into the dark.

Lucky Strikes

One day he steps out for a pack of smokes
And comes back to find his family has deserted *him*.
The wife with the endcurled hair, the boy and the girl
And even his mother, who'd come to live with them
After Pops died: *poof.* This is all happening
In black and white. Everything's silvery gray.
So he pours himself a drink and lights a cigarette.
He smokes aggressively, slams down his scotch.
Now he's holding an empty glass, staring into space
That separates him from me and you. What in the world
Could he be thinking? That this is all a dream,
That it's somebody else's life? Uh-uh. The unreality
Of the existence that consumed him has been replaced,
He sees, by something all too familiar: the reality
He'd feared, those moments of deep introspection
When he'd wondered how it all came to be, marveled
At it, and felt a little guilty. He always knew
What ought to happen, and now it has. A little strange,
Like coming come, things as they should be.
He hops in his convertible and drives out to a nightclub
On the strand. He's heard about the torch singer
Working here, a beautiful svelte woman with a smoky voice.
He'll sit at the bar and listen to her songs about love.
Watching it all diminish, the whiskey and filter kings.
Something sharp and raw that arrives with a pleasurable pain
And leaves gracefully, curling upwards in tall lingering wisps.

Demitasse

The dregs puddling in our cups
And the taste of imported cigarettes
Growing stale in our mouths
Matched exquisitely
The afternoon's grainy half-light.
Paper trash bumped along the street
And the waiter dropped a tray of saucers
In the kitchen. Like a train in the subway
It came on suddenly even though
Anticipated, as mute and real
As the table under its cloth,
And left only the fact of you,
Your ash-blond hair,
The smudged imprint of your lips.

Postcoital

It was late in the ironic age, and everywhere
Poets in baggy jeans and heavy work shoes
Sprawled wide-legged about the public squares,
Smoking cigarettes and speaking openly
Of their lovers' genitalia. Some called it

The crucible of human anatomy, a dark,
Hooded figure, cloaked in the wattled,
Hirsute robes of the lesser clergy. And,
As you might have guessed, it was all
About death, and there was something in it

Of the self, and since, as no one could deny,
The allegorical possibilities were endless,
They simply went on forever. And so
A whole church sprang up around it,
And the scriptures described the laying on

Of hands, how one might cup it under palm
And curled fingers or part its delicate cowl
With a deft thumb tip. The sacraments
Included a Eucharist, and the poets' work,
Generally performed live, was rife

With allusions to it, references to how
They took the host into their mouths,
Held it on their tongues, and washed it

Down with a wine more rare than the spilt
Blood of anyone who might never have

Even lived. They prayed often, these poets,
Getting down on their knees, heads bowed.
But never, as it turned out, in the open. Before
Other people, they laughed, smoked their cigarettes,
And jeered at the nonbelievers; ate only saltines

And drank wine from screw-top bottles.

Stevens in a Swarm of Gnats

The man wearing the tailored suit, casually
Overdressed: in the midst of this confusion
He loses track (though not direction, bearing,

Altitude). It may be he loses faith
In his loss of faith. Maybe never. Perhaps,
As with everything, he always had it. But these

Tiny, dark, annoying, air-scribbling, vaguely
Malicious *things* keep buzzing around him like
Electrons about a nucleus, interstellar debris

In manic orbit around some host planet,
Equally attracted and repelled by its gravity,
Product of its mass—until, somewhere beyond

Desperation, he resolves to do nothing more
Than grin and bear it. He is clumsy, he knows:
A great, hulking giant standing out of doors

(There in the flower garden probably,
Beyond the hemlocks, among the hollyhocks),
Having removed himself from all enclosures,

His eyes and ears uncovered, quite open,
Nostrils even slightly flared, come what may.
He's given up on battening down the hatches,

Accepts, resignedly, whatever niggling invader
Happens to penetrate his gnostic shell,
Through now with all his languid waving away,

Content *just to be there, just to be beheld,*
Hazed into submission, enveloped, beclouded,
Consumed, finally, in this particulate fog.

Variations on a Theme by Nietzsche

Have you heard? Now Mildred is dead. Her shrunken head,
Kept for its likeness, lies half-deflated on a coffee table.
The cleaning woman lifts it to dust, plumps it like a pillow,
Puts it back. O Mildred! Eighty-four, just arriving.

And Klaus is dead, even as K.525 circles endlessly in stereo.
The night droops on its curtain rod, the moon, sad-sacked
As Mildred's head, faintly glowing, tumbles lumpily
Among low hills. Mata Hari is dead. La Rochefoucault.

The ghost of Francois Villon has been arrested and jailed.
I think Lewis Mumford might be dead, though I'm not sure
Who he was. But Louise Brooks, Valentino. Miss Manners.
Dead are Borges and Bishop, Paul Klee and Cassius Clay, Bergen

And McCarthy. Your mother and father might be dead.
How long has it been since you looked? Sisters and brothers,
Aunts and uncles, all your cousins. It looks like winter
In your family tree. Even the buzzards humped on its limbs

Aren't looking well, and you can tell which way
They'll be going. Dead are Carlos and Cynthia, Hamish
And Martha, Frank and Alice. The man who sold pictures
At the fair. Bill, Sue, John, Fred. All dead. Who can doubt it.

The rivers are readying themselves to exit into the sea.
Anxiety, at last, has fled. The wind howls and ocean waves
Keep crashing against the beaches, no one there to see them.
The sky pours out its color, clouds are herded into chutes.

Deftly Stilled

I. View of Delft
    after Jan Vermeer

The city stares, facing piles staid as stumps,
        Partially veiled in a partial gloom,
    Glowing at its heart—the rowed
        Roofs like fresh-fired terra-cotta pots up-

Turned—paved, tiled, half-timbered, high-pitched, gate-mouthed
        And bulwark-walled, slabbed and stuccoed,
    Reflecting on itself
        In pewter-like inland-waterway water

Where wait broad-beamed, heavy-hulled cargo boats,
        Tied up like oxen, to take on wares;
    Across the way, some towns-
        People, hooded, hatted, properly bleak

In puritanical black, convene, converse,
        Oblivious to the opulently radiant
    Sunlit spire of the Nieuwe
        Kerk—"burial place of the Princes of Orange

And the city's symbolic core"—raised apparently
        Toward a fortuitous hole in a heaven
    Mottled with marbled clouds,
        Soft, soft-white, and gray, likes stones in mortar.

II. View of Delft with a Musical Instrument Dealer
after Carel Fabritius

A city-surrounded church, the Nieuwe Kerk:
    Canal, cobblestone street, and corbie-
  Step façade, footbridge, fount,
      And space itself seeming to sweep around

Its gothic gargantuaness, as if, to show
    Its rear, it painted a self-portrait
  In a convex mirror, back-
      Wards; "shortly after the crypt beneath the tomb

Of William the Silent was opened to receive
    The body of William II," and owing
  To the gravity of the whole
      Affair, it wished to convey front and center

Some sense of the city's centripetal movement,
    Throwing in, for symmetry's sake,
  This contemplative member
      Of the mercantile, vandyked Dutch dandy

Cavalierly capped, coated, and cuffed,
    Thumb to chin, lute and bass viol beside,
  Bemused, his gaze just grazing
      The arch perimeter of its frozen music.

Vermeer's Window

To see you in the corner of a room
    Reading a letter, say, or balancing scales,
Or just letting the light strike you, affords
    A kind of compensation, a world complete.

You might be seated at a table, wearing
    Your fine yellow jacket made of satin.
The white pitcher with the pewter lid could be
    Before you, and there might be someone else,

A confidant, someone through whom someone else
    Might pass you a folded note that says, "I love
How light refracts, genuflects, coming through glass,
    And, in regarding your face, submits to doing

Only this." She'd probably stand between you
    And a map of the known world, this friend of yours,
A faded map on cracking parchment, held flat
    On the back wall by an iron bar attached

To give it weight. You wouldn't speak, the two
    Of you, not while I was watching, of course,
But something more might pass, which I could sense
    Arcing across the quiet room at light

Speed: the answer, for instance, to the question
    Of how the simple act of seeing you
Writing a letter, say, or fingering pearls,
    Could prove, conclusively, that light is all

The eye can know. The window, mattering much,
    Would seem somehow to comprehend all this,
And to keep the room arranged just so: the table
    There, there the pitcher, the wall, the old map.

Burne-Jones, in the National Gallery, Views *The Arnolfini Marriage* One Last Time

Sunday of Beauvais was the first day of creation
    and the day I first saw Gabriel
would be another—and there are six—and the seventh day
    is any day when I see you. But
what are you doing this day . . . who is daring
    to look at you—is he worthy
of seeing you—is he worthy of living on the same
    green ball of an earth? Don't answer,
please don't. I couldn't bear you to speak
    your mind, couldn't bear you
to suddenly glare back at me like the ghastly face
    in the shaving mirror that has haunted
my dreams for years. I keep thinking of the first
    sight of you—and why it's not you
who comes in dreams to me instead of the other—
    but I still see those divine little figures
moving in a land no man ever saw, in a light
    none can dream of—better than Italy sun
ever did. I had a glimpse of what a heaven life
    could be—of sustained ecstasy
at visible beauty—and I've sustained myself on it
    all this time. No disaster can touch you now
and my happiness hangs on a little thread. Isn't it great
    to be made like that? Such strength as yours

I see nowhere and I mind for you more than for
     anyone, yet the day I go you will lose
nothing. Once, it looked as if we had just the same thoughts
     about all things. The invisible seed
was growing. Sometimes in the depths I've known
     yours was the better fate, but on the crest
of the wave I thought mine the best—only it is so
     short-lived on the crest, and the trough
is so deep and long. A certain kind of silly rubbish
     has always helped me—deep down we are all
face to face with a certain solemnity—we can guess
     that much—so I shall be silly till you want me
to be sad, and then you shall have all the sadness
     that is in me . . . whether I see you or not.

A Palace for the Heart

Just after Ludwig II's death the surgeons opened
    below his ribs and removed his heart.
It's now preserved, indeed enshrined, in a silver vase
    "of French design," and said to rest
in Altötting's Votive Chapel, watched over by
    the "famous miraculous" Black Madonna;
and, perversely curious reading this, I soon pass over
    the question of *why* and turn instead
to wondering *how* exactly his heart resides in there:
    did they leave it to simply slip and slump
into some slouched position? Or is it mounted
    somehow? Propped up? Is it enthroned?
Also, are the hearts of royalty pre-drained? Or
    does the fluid pool, congeal, dry up,
in the bottom's basin? Ridiculous really, when you see
    the big picture: a man decanting
in suburbia, pondering the fate of an inner organ
    long stopped, a continent away
(not his anyway), enthralled, engrossed, in need
    of more than blocks on blocks in La-
La Land. Outside, the garden miles, partitioned lawns
    and sculptured hedges, screaming out,
"We *are* the bourgeoisie!" while a wretched regiphile
    like me just keeps on sinking, couched
in bloated biographies, revealing all but what
    one wants to know. But, oh, all right,
let's hear it all about the King's alleged fling

with Richard Wagner, nationalism,
insanity; but, please, get on with it, and on
  to something *edifying*. Yes,
get to the heart of Ludwig's matter: residency.
  Let's glimpse his life in *Linderhof:*
evenings afloat in his tiny solo shell-shaped boat
  (the lake alit by electric lights!)
in the man-made grotto. Of storm-dense afternoons
  a thorough study ought to explain
how the King climbed *Neuschwanstein's* tower to watch
  the way rivers into real lakes drain,
alone perhaps, but *gemütlich* and alpinely amused;
  or isolate on an island in
an inland lake in the Louis *Schloss, Herrenchiemsee,*
  that graceful palace of French design:
as I envision the scene, the King has quietly slipped
  out through the secret-passage door
from his dressing room to the place he most likes to be,
  at ease in a cordate-back settee,
a lounging figure swathed in silk, content to drown
  in cushions stuffed with eiderdown.

My Work with the King

Georg von Dollmann, Ludwig's architect

I. *Linderhof*

We could have finished had he kept his mind
to this, a solitary gem, its mount
near Oberammergau, the home of wood-
carvers and Passion plays, of edelweiss,
and *Lederhosen'd* peasants who loved the King.
They stage Christ's suffering, his death and res-
urrection, decennially, but these same
young men—a Son of God, a dozen disciples,
thieves, Romans, whores, et cetera—keep Ludwig's
picture pinned to their peasant-bloused chests
every day as they tramp about the woods
surrounding *Linderhof.*
                            Their mountain idyll,
it features terraced cascades carved in hillsides,
a fountain which on the hour lifts, lifts, lifts, and holds
a shaft of water a hundred feet above
the stroller's head (high enough, I suppose,
for even the walled-out peasants to see),
magnificent rooms, a Moorish kiosk, and a man-
made grotto with lake illuminated blue
by lights below the water. Floating above:
a tiny boat in the shape of a giant shell
and scenes from *Tannhäuser* on the lighted walls.
A recess indeed for the weary.

Still, some ask,
Is this fit place for a king, a man of state,
in a shell-shaped boat on an artificial lake?
But I've seen him there, on summer afternoons
when Munich is all heat, dust, and close air,
and even in the Alps the sky reflects
the paved bustle of cities: and so I tell
them, "Yes, from here a king may truly govern,
(if only peasants trained for parts in heaven)."

II. *Neuschwanstein*

Capricious castle piercing the clouds
above the valley of the swans,
beloved fortress—it was built
by men, who for the time it took,
dwelt in worlds other than their own.
Indeed, it may become the model
for men who would spin deceptive webs
for children.
                              Ludwig grew up just
below in the family's alpine stronghold,
Schloss Hohenschwangau, whose stone blocks
are softened, held in check, by vines
relentlessly scaling its outer walls;
its chambers spellbound by frescoes
of Lohengrin's arrival at Antwerp,
his skiff drawn by a swan, maid Elsa's
deliverance from Telramund. . . .

I think it's safe to say he never
escaped that romance.

                    Years later, *insane,*
he was reciting lines from Schiller—
Don Carlos—"in a very loud voice,"
when Doctor Gudden came to call.
His henchmen were with him, burghers from
the Crown Council carrying a straight-
jacket. But peasants of the valley
got wind of the plot and armed themselves
with axes, knives, and stones to guard
their unsuspecting King, locked in
drama in the Minnesinger Hall.
The villains were quickly apprehended,
Füssen's honorable magistrate summoned,
and once the doctor had time to explain,
he and his bunch were tossed in the clink—
straight off! I've always had a deep
appreciation for Schiller myself:
fast-paced action, poetic justice.

III. *Herrenchiemsee*

Built on the Herreninsel, a wooded island
in the middle of a lake, this yet unfin-
nished palace attempts to reproduce *Versailles*:
its gardens draw and frame with leaves and flowers;
its drawing rooms are gardens of fleurs-de-lis;
and even the hall of mirrors mimics its model,

dripping and dancing with light. We only lacked
some Louis (marks and francs!) to make our court
complete. The isle itself, enchanted thing,
crisscrossed this way and that by woodland paths
exquisite for walks in summer, is a place
of shade and mystery. Arriving there,
the King directed us to light some torches
and place them on the broader trails. He dressed
his servants (including me) as the footmen of
French kings, then later, in the darkest hours,
emerged as Louis XIV!
                                    On an island
in a lake, the middle of night: our King was swallowed
whole by dreams, visions. Taking a carriage ride
in grand French gear, beneath the forest limbs,
through dusky smells, now faint, now blazing light
of torches, we paraded paths till dawn. . . .
The final irony, construction ended
with a watery image: having drowned the doctor,
the King tried reaching the opposite shore,
perceiving safety in its gleaming castle,
but found himself, alas, unsuited for swimming.

The Morning's News

Otto von Bismarck, Imperial Chancellor

In point of fact, I couldn't be more pleased
to learn that certain royals drowned. Why not
Princess Victoria, for instance, found
floating face-down (O bottoms up!) in the bath . . .
But a quip not fit for publication.
I must coin one now. Let's see, what have I
yet said . . . O yes: *Either the King is sane,*
in which case he will do as I suggest,
or he is really mad, and then he won't . . .
Or something very like it. Anyway,
I should be safe as far as Munich goes,
with both the beer Philistines and the King's
survivors. Diplomacy demands but that
you never call them foolish to their faces.

Samuel Langhorne Clemens, the writer and humorist Mark Twain

You never call them foolish to their faces
and fools may fail to get the point. Why, here
sweet fortune grants Bavarians their chance
to oust the throne, and them too cowardly
to do the job. But be that as it may,
let one king drown in a "tiny, inland lake"
and I shall swim in oceans of satisfaction!
There's only this to impede my celebration:
on finding himself lampooned in *Tramp Abroad,*
I'm told His Royal Extravagancy

came near laughing a hole in his silken breeches—
a finer show of character than most
republicans can claim. And next to us
the King appeared more natural in clothes.

Elisabet Ney, German-American sculptress

The King appeared more natural in clothes
than crude newspaper drawings can convey.
And that they show him hauled in from the lake
like a bearded eel in a silk waistcoat!
Admittedly though, as a nude he'd look
sillier still: that tiny wing-topped head
rolling around atop those broad shoulders,
like a pea balanced on a butter knife.
Lucky for me my commission was to cast
a Youthful Sovereign in Grand Master's robes.
Later, it might have been Mature Monarch
in French finery, face sunken with loss
of teeth from eating candy. . . . Truer though:
so much blunter is the pain which comes through.

Hans von Bülow, composer/conductor

So much blunter is the pain which comes through
reading the papers: first, I learn my wife
has given birth to Wagner's son, and thus
is crowned, in the most resplendent fashion,
the high edifice of my cuckoldom;
then, later comes the news of Wagner's death,
which, heaven help me, wounds more deeply yet;

now this! Having been taxed with, already,
the infamy of accepting the most
disgraceful bargain as a favorite
of a favorite of the King—in God's
name, what am I now? Pray there is no term
for it a journalist may use. I fear
nothing but what tomorrow's papers bring!

Victoria, Queen of England

Nothing but what tomorrow's papers bring
shall yet surprise us. Albert, *Mein Liebchen*,
do not allow such travesties disturb
your rest. Which presently reminds:
what mode of dress is proper for a prince
at times like this? *Direct his valet lay
out on his bed the suit best fitting us
our degree of mourning. We are shocked, of course . . .*
And must have more particulars. . . . *Send wire:
the Queen demands to know details!* For all
that comes to mind's my memory of him,
that once we met: standing before me, stock
still, speaking with utmost solemnity,
his eyes tightly shut for the duration. . . .

Rudolf, Crown Prince of Austria

His eyes tightly shut for the duration,
I'll wager, groping blindly towards it,
afraid to see, the famous *King of Midnight*
embarking on a journey darker yet—

and riding tandem! Given that, how to
regard this, we who contemplate the art
of *Selbstmord*? An unforeseen complication?
A tactical blunder? Breach of etiquette?
Or masterstroke, confusing, as it does,
the means by which he passed, creating doubt
and mystery . . . and a traveling companion
with whom to board that gruesome ferry. Ludwig:
always the family's foolish ineffectual—
and yet to prove of what he was capable!

Sophie, Duchess of Alençon

And yet to prove of what he was capable
after all—after all but leaving me
standing at the altar, precipitating
my fall from Europe's most enviable
to most pitiable "would-be" in one fell
swoop of his clumsy, fidgeting, overly
precious prerogative! Though I'll admit,
it saved me untold future embarrassment,
excuses to his royal dinner guests,
lies of explanation for his behavior,
the shame of scandal for his taking lovers
(who weren't even other women!). Yes, I
should have been thankful then and saddened now.
In point of fact, I couldn't be more pleased.

The Gardener's Tale

Karl von Effner, director of the royal gardens

Midsummer, east parterre:
a scene inspired by—what? Pythagoras?
       Nothing in nature is
   like this: calculated to please
   simply for the sake of pleasing.
Ludwig loved it—of course,
not as much as the Winter Garden, but
       then, that's a portable
   pleasance, imported (or rather,
   dis-Oriented) from places
as far east as Persia
and the precincts of Patusan—potted,
       pruned, and presented un-
   der glass. We procured palms, peacocks,
   pagodas, poppies, peonies,
and parti-colored blooms
of every possible shape, size, and form
       —not to mention a pair
   of gazelles and a prized parrot
   that reproduced so perfectly
Ludwig's loud, nervous laugh,
footmen hearing it perked up in panic
       at their Master's unex-
   pected presence. One fall, we packed
   it all up and shipped it to *Schloss*
Berg on Starnbergersee—
palms, peafowl, plants, and all—and all for a

princess! (oh, all right then,
a grand duchess, one Maria
of Russia, or St. Petersburg
to be precise, where match-
makers prate, pander, and peddle their wares).
Most thought—especially
the girl's mother, a czarina—
Ludwig would fall prostrate before
Her Pouting Prettiness;
but—and about this I take a certain,
how shall I say . . . *perverse*
pleasure—His Majesty showed less
interest in the Duchess than in
my premier progeny:
Peter! You see, the elder boy was there
to help unpack, de-pot,
replant, et cetera, and the King just
happened to notice him reposed
upon a peat pallet,
parched and perspiring heavily, his shirt
pasted like a poultice
to his chest and back. Ludwig paused,
and I, heart palpitating, feared
a reprimand, perhaps
some painful punishment for having pooped
out before Paradise
was . . . recompleted, so to speak;
but no! Nothing of the kind. No,
it seems the King had stopped
to ask, merely to ask, about a par-

ticular type of plant,
wanting to know if it was not
indeed some kind of a pansy. . . .
Ah, the large part that luck
plays in our precious lives: this, *this*, was
a prime example, for
you see, it so happens Peter
is an expert on this flower,
a hybrid, the purplest
of purples, its petals plush as velvet.
Presently, they were off,
perambulating the lake shore,
each delighted with the other's
genius and unmistak-
able perspicacity regarding
things horticultural.
And to my paternal delight,
this meeting was but the prelude
to a longer, deeper
relationship, which, upon our return
to the Palace, reached full
blossom: the King, notorious
insomniac that he was, was
soon calling for Peter
every night! Before long, they were insep-
arable. As for me,
well, I could not have been more proud.
But, of course, into every tale
comes some conflict. In this
case the forms were pettiness, jealousy,

and pernicious gossip:
you see, some said their love was not . . .
platonic (my Greek, not theirs), but
sordid, sinful, at best
pathetic. And I'm ashamed to say that,
at first, I allowed it
to cause me a good deal of pain.
But this too soon passed and was re-
placed, posthaste, by pride. (And
would that I not fall prey again
to such prude perversions,
perpetrated by those priggish
pillars of pettiness!) You see,
two points of fact prevailed:
one, Munich produces many bright boys,
but the King chose mine; and
two, many and varied are love's
productions transposed by the Greeks!

Invective Against Swan Songs

King Otto, Ludwig's brother/successor,
from the insane asylum

The soul, good people, flies beyond the parks
And far beyond the domes of the winter palace.

Waking in a strange, phosphorescent light,
It rises, deliberate, and goes without saying

Like a sleepwalker summoned by the moon
To carry out a nobler office. Snow

Falls silently, and the owl's downy wings
Make no sound as it swings through the cold night.

Behold, already on the long parades
The carrion birds descend to line the streets.

And the soul, good people, having lately risen
Escapes the walls of speech as another prison.

IV

More Reading Habits

for Graham

His son has become a great lover of books
And is just now tearing through his first novel:
The Brothers Karamazov. He's six months old,
A prodigy in diapers seated on the floor.
Ripping along page after page, he curls
The deconstructed fragments in his fingers,
Waves them overhead to see how they fly,
Then sticks them in his mouth, chews, savoring
The complex flavors that survive his translation.
Pausing, reflective, he decides for himself
Whether to swallow the story or to spit it out,
For he's already a connoisseur, a shrewd
Poststructuralist founding his own school.
And there, at the table, is Pops, Daddy, Old
Blood and Guts, heaped over his platters,
Trying to digest what happens to the father
In this tale, buffoon who gets, alas, what he deserves.

For the Drowned

First, the river unclothes them, washes
Toward the Gulf their t-shirts and tennis shoes,
Their torn khakis and simple housedresses,
And even, eventually, the finer points
Of their faces, the identifying features,
So that, often, they seem to arrive incomplete,
Like lumps of clay not yet fully formed,
Flesh unpronounceable. Arturo says it's fish—
Mudcats and alligator gars—that take what's
Missing. They'll eat anything, he says,
And I imagine as much with each rising bubble
In the draft. We find ten or twelve a year,
And all of them aliens, illegals, wetbacks.
Or so it goes in the reports. Who knows?
Who can tell by looking? Here in The Valley,
Our tongues are already swollen with two languages,
The contents of our stomachs is the same,
And most of us are too poor for dentists.
But it makes life less complicated for the coroner.
The county's reserved a special place for them
In the graveyard. He applies the tags. Arturo and I
Backhoe the graves out of dirt too thin for planting,
Inter the bodies, reclothed, faceless in white bags.

Dichotomies

In the dream of the perfectly symmetrical universe
he sees himself in love with that special someone
created just for him: for every boy, a girl

or another boy, for every girl, a girl or boy.
Of course, there isn't an ounce of truth in this—
he's never seen a perfect pair, not one—but he

can't help thinking about it the morning of his first
prostate exam, after the nurse checks his pulse
and before the doctor comes. She's young, perky.

She has a mild overbite he finds charming, and it seems
it might align itself precisely with his prognathic jaw.
Could this be her? Could she be the one? He compares her

to his wife, whom he's loved in a desultory sort of way
for some eleven years now. Just look at her, she's so well
balanced! And she understands him, he can tell by the way

she holds her pen. He invents a scenario that lands them
in love: unable to ignore their fate they give in to passion
and determine to meet at a secluded spot beside the lake.

The nurse, it turns out, has a travel trailer, because, like him,
she loves the outdoors. They fling off their clothes
and open the RV's flimsy window curtains—they want

to see the tree limbs bowing gracefully over the water
while they screw. The dining table unfolds neatly
into a twin-size bed and as they lie on it she explains

how they're completely justified in being there. They're
two parts of a whole, she says, and she may even
make reference to Eastern philosophy, though he doesn't

let his creamy daydream bog down in its own details.
He cuts to the good part: propelled by their innocent
lust they make love on the eggcrate mattress, finding

that everything fits just so and there's no reason
for awkwardness to come between them. They climax
simultaneously just as the doctor inserts a greased

laytex-gloved finger into his ass. In his mind, they moan
in unison. And the doctor says, "Oh, does that hurt? Are you
tender there?" He wakes from his daydream. And so it goes

with pivotal moments. He feels divided, the nurse leaves
the room. He asks himself, Is this the life or is it only
some notion of a life? Can I face the face in the mirror,

and can the mirror be trusted? I don't look the same
in pictures. My voice, so well modulated as it comes out
of my mouth, sounds, on tape, like opera interpreted on kazoo.

So this is the world, he thinks, poleaxed into conflicting
hemispheres. Dark and light, good and evil, perception
and reality—ha! Would that it were so simple! Would that he

could make such arithmetical sense of things! Leaving
the doctor's office, he notices how strangely he's walking
and remembers, last winter, splitting logs with a maul

and wedge before shoving them into the glory hole of his pot-
bellied stove. They splintered and cracked and, in the end,
burned down to homogenous ash, gray, silty, insubstantial.

What is it that happens to them in their burning, so urgent
and penetrating, that they can never be whole again, and are left
there only to be swept up, scattered, buried, dispersed?

Valley of You

The moon pours down its vaporous milk, and below her,
The night's furtive waves form a ribbon of foam.
Yes, you have seen to her pasture,
But one fence is a cliff and it overlooks the sea,
One is a road and it leads to the north,
And her barn is just a stand of trees
Where a winding darkness swirls in the rafters.
Who could have guessed that even the blades of grass
Could not be trusted and would choose this moment
To whisper in her ear? She whips her tail
And sends ripples of portent riding off through the night.
You are in your farmhouse, and you are sleeping,
When they enter the attic. You think they are ghosts
And shiver in your bed. And then,
Turning to your wife, hoping for the best,
You slide one leg next to hers, place one hand on her hair.
But when it is over, you know that you will feel alone,
And it will still be dark. And then that plaintive lowing:
A rich contralto that flows, like sorghum, over the fields,
Calling you, as it might to anyone, to come, carefully
Warming your hands, and kneel there beside her.

Municipal Airport

Because we love to taxi

Because the sun seems brighter here

Because the tarmac is a gleaming expanse

Because the runway is longer and wider than we should ever need

Because it begins and ends with cryptic numbers

Because they chart the bearings of our soul

Because the fuselage trembles at full throttle

Because the propeller spins and its motion is in a circle

Because the circle is perfect

Because it asks us to believe in our delicate wings

Because they hold us aloft with their clever deflections

Because we call it a cockpit

Because we call it a cabin

Because we pack ourselves into it

Because we peer out of it through glass that wraps itself around us

Because the earth falls gracefully away from us

Because we begin to see it as the body of our lover

Because we know we will fall back to it

Because either way our return will be glorious

Because it will leave us exhausted and happy

Because it won't be our death they remember here

Because they will have the good sense to ignore it

Outing

I should have known as soon as I saw the note,
Pinned to a piling, bent double in the breeze,
Things were not going to go as I had planned.
Across the cove, bellbuoys clanged *Distance*,
Desire, and I glanced once over the lake. The sun's heat
Radiating from the dock's wooden planks,
Its light glinting on the folds of wavelets
And, reflected, swimming like copper fishes
Across the watermarked paper: *Go ahead, out in*
The boat. Lie back on the gunwale at deep anchor.
See how in sunlight sunlight is all and is enough.

Bio

As a child she loved color and played forget-me-not
In the garden. High school was a cult of one
And she changed her name to Gladdis,
Sweeter than the sound. She went to college,
Kept a scrapbook, later blossomed. Admittedly,
However, she was eventually deflowered.
Forced, then, to go underground, she holed up
In the dark, and when finally she emerged,
It was night, so no one was watching.
She derived great pleasure from admiring shadows
She cast while standing naked under the moon.
But like all things this too came to an end
And she wound up working days in a coffee shop,
Keeping an eye on the cash drawer. At some point
She was put out to pasture where she spent her time
In the heated exchange of decomposition. Presently,
She's in the roses. Her lilacs are in love
With hydrangeas. She is found, during taste tests,
To linger like foxglove. And when paper whites
Are in soft sun she breathes, like a florid sigh,
Her only answer. Her goal is to go on working forever.

Bluebonnets

Sing for me
Tumultuous field
Your own trembling
Arpeggios

There's something violet
At the heart of me
Something green
Beneath my skin

Scratch it, peel it back
Break a branch of me
Not yet hollow
And sing for me

O sing, sing
Be my voice
Rising, turning
In yellow air.

Between Ice Ages

What you'll notice first are the trees,
Black ironwork against a backdrop
Of snow, and beyond them the house,

Alone in this white-carpeted world
Like the last specimen of a breed
Before extinction. How shall we hunker

Down, with only so much firewood,
So much meat in the locker,
And so many stories left

To which we can still bear to listen?
Let's wander outdoors until we're standing
In those same woods, just back

From somewhere it took us a long time
To go. See the house, its chimney smoke?
Come closer still, rest on my shoulder,

Let me tell you about the snowman
We built one year. In the depths
Of his milky opalescence lurked a pure

Lethean blue, a cold blue. He was
Really something, or so we thought. Quite
The stoic, the steadfast guardian,

Even at night. And beautiful,
To us anyway. But there was this,
How he didn't melt, and didn't, and then,

When he did, went so quietly,
Unnoticed, unremarked, and so
Deliberately, that we learned to forget,

In tiny increments, he was ever there.

The Novel of Grisly Details

Now, in this late-afternoon sinking, the lakeshore
May remind you of a magnificent city

Brought to ruin: the talus of silt-stained rocks,
Those leggy weeds strewn up the hill—and the waves,

How they lap against it, listlessly, as if they
Didn't care. Soon, we'll hear from the bullfrogs.

Insects will emerge to grind away the night.
The barge of shadow will slide over us like the lid

Of a sepulcher, and then we'll have the spectacle
Of a million eyes watching us from right here

Inside our dusty, drafty little crypt. Supplanted
By a taste for the artificial, the colder and less

Illuminating, what we will lose is something
Traded away for comfort. What we'll miss most

Is that which we paid dearest to give away.
Remember the porch light. Remember to lock

The door. Remember, before turning out the lamp,
To set the alarm, and to remind yourself to wake

With a renewed sense of the inevitable.
Remember to mark your place in the story.

Notes

"Burne-Jones, in the National Gallery, Views *The Arnolfini Marriage* One Last Time": specific language for this poem was adapted from the artist's letters quoted in *Edward Burne-Jones: a Biography*, by Penelope Fitzgerald (London: Joseph, 1975).

Section III: the poems in this section are taken from a book-length manuscript on Ludwig II of Bavaria. I have long felt that everything about Ludwig II cries out for poetic treatment: his life, his work, his "building projects," his patronage of Richard Wagner, and, especially perhaps, his mysterious death. And the fact is I consider the subject closely allied to my own youthful experiences because I moved to West Germany (as an Army brat) at age twelve and, after visiting Neuschwanstein, became devoted to the legend of "The Mad King." I toured the castle and Ludwig's other residences on several occasions. Since that time, I have read everything about him I could get my hands on (which becomes part of the thematic development of the poem "A Palace for the Heart"). And I continue to see Ludwig as an intensely poetic subject, devoted to the arts, devoted to his own romantic visions and view of life, handsome, intelligent, eccentric, morbid, at times cruel and hateful, in the end, tragic. In these and other respects I think his life speaks eloquently to us across the divide of some 115 years—on the primacy of art, for instance, and on the dangers of public adulation. Through the voices of a number of his survivors, I take as my starting point his death, look backward at his life, his lineage, his emerging legend. My hope was to make each of the poems stand on its own merit, though admittedly they fare better when taken in the aggregate.

"A Palace for the Heart": another example of how the facts of Ludwig's life are stranger than the legends. Something about this detail struck me as worthy of poetic treatment—that they should encase the hearts of the royal family, entomb them separately from the rest of the body, keep them in ornate vases on shelves in a designated chapel. Ironic, considering Ludwig's repeated attempts to procure lodgings he found suitable to his romantic notions, that in the end he should find, if the reader will forgive me this, that "home is where the heart is."

"My Work with the King": Ludwig continues to be best known for his castles, especially Neuschwantstein, one of the most visited tourist attractions in the world and the model for Disney's castle. Georg von Dollman was only one of several architects to work with Ludwig. In the end, he was blamed for problems incurred during construction—including the exorbitant costs—fired, and relegated to a position of national shame. None of the castles was ever completed, though Linderhof came close.

"The Morning's News": Ludwig had been one of the most famous reigning monarchs in the world. Verlaine, in a famous poem, called him the century's only real king. But by the time of his death in 1886, he had many enemies in his own country. The peasants still loved him, but the burghers of Munich thought he was either crazy or such a megalomaniac that his removal from the throne was necessary to maintain, among other things, Bavaria's economic stability. The Crown Council had the most highly regarded psychiatrist in the country, Dr. Bernhard von Gudden, to declare Ludwig insane, though the doctor had never actually even examined the King and based his diagnosis solely on the reports of those who had been called to give secret testimony. At any rate, after von Gudden and company captured Ludwig, they transferred him from Neuschwanstein to Schloss Berg, on Lake Starnberger, there to keep an eye on him until the Crown Council could decide its next move. A few days into his confinement, Ludwig and the doctor went for a walk by the lake. They never returned. Their bodies were later found floating in shallow water, von Gudden's near the shore, Ludwig's about twenty yards out. And thus, Ludwig's legend, already substantial, grew enormous. Speculation persists to this day about what happened. The peasants always maintained that the two men were murdered. Others have conjectured that it was the result of a failed attempt to liberate Ludwig from his captors. Most people believe, however, that the King, a strong swimmer, had simply planned to swim to freedom, von Gudden tried to stop him, and Ludwig, a much larger man, in the process of fighting him off, strangled the good doctor to death. Exhausted, then, from the struggle, he drowned after managing to cover only a short distance. Divots and gouges in the turf near the shore and bruise marks on von Gudden's face and neck seem to support this theory. News of the event quickly circled the globe, and in the poems in this sequence I imagine the responses of various people who would have had some personal or intellectual interest in the story.

—Otto von Bismarck: the record shows that through Bismarck's shrewd and somewhat underhanded statesmanship—and through Ludwig's own weakness—the Iron Chancellor was able to wrest from our hero the sovereignty of Bavaria through his authorship of the so-called *Kaiserbrief*, a letter he wrote and, via one of Ludwig's own ministers, persuaded the King to put his name to, in effect giving away the country his family had ruled for over 700 years. In truth, it was probably just a matter of time before Bavaria was overwhelmed by the Bismarck Juggernaut anyway.

—Samuel Longhorne Clemens: see the 1996 Oxford University Press edition of *A Tramp Abroad*, pp. 97-99. The story about Ludwig's delight in the passage, read to him by someone on his staff, is true.

—Elisabet Ney: this noted artist, whose statues of Sam Houston and Stephen F. Austin are on display in the foyer of the Texas state capitol in Austin, has the distinction of creating the only likeness of Ludwig he himself ever liked. Wanting to reward Ney for the success of her endeavors, he offered to send her "a collection" of jewels and let her choose what she pleased. She replied that she had "no time to care for jewels" and that her friends always gave her flowers. Ludwig had a carriage load of exotic blooms from his own conservatories sent to her the next day, and every succeeding day until her work on his statue was completed. See *The Art of the Woman: The Life and Work of Elisabet Ney*, by Emily Fourmy Cutrer. Lincoln: University of Nebraska Press, 1988. pp. 74-75.

—Hans von Bülow: so devoted to Wagner was this noted conductor that even after the scandal of his wife's affair with the illustrious composer he continued to worship him and to conduct his operas. He and Cosima eventually divorced and she married Wagner, but not before the scandal had become a politically damaging embarrassment for Ludwig, and the cause of public humiliation for von Bülow.

—Victoria: see Lytton Strachey's famous biography with regard to the Queen's continuing to have Prince Albert's clothes laid out for him every evening for the forty years that remained to her after his death. (New York: Harcourt Brace, 1921. p. 404.) The poem's details concerning the one meeting between Ludwig and Victoria, a distant cousin, are also taken straight from the biographies.

—Rudolf: son of Emperor Franz Josef and Empress Elizabeth and Ludwig's first cousin, from his youth the Crown Prince was devoted to his famously romantic relative and the two of them spent a fair amount of time together. As Rudolf grew older and began to despair of his father's ever dying so he could ascend to the throne, he began to rebel publicly against the Emperor's reactionary world view and distanced himself from everyone in the family, including Ludwig. Three years after Ludwig's death, in what became one of the most shocking scandals and pathetic tragedies of the age, Rudolf and his mistress committed joint suicide. The subject of the Claude Anet novel, *Mayerling* (after the name of the location where the lovers killed themselves), the story has been adapted for film some five or six times, once, in 1936, with Charles Boyer playing Rudolf, and once, in 1968, with Omar Sharif in the role and Catherine Deneuve in the role of his mistress.

—Sophie: sister of Empress Elizabeth, she enjoyed a brief period as the fiancée of the most eligible bachelor in Europe, if not the world. But outside of Elizabeth herself, whom Ludwig adored and considered the one person with whom he had the closest spiritual bond, the young King had virtually no romantic interest in women and after a series of embarrassing and public faux pas on his part, the engagement ended.

"The Gardener's Tale": most of the details about the garden, and the details about the Czarina's visit, are true. The rest I made up.

"Invective Against Swan Songs": in another of the remarkable ironies of the story, Ludwig was ousted from the throne on the pretense that he was insane. His resulting death meant that, technically, the throne of Bavaria now passed to his younger brother, Otto, who had been in an insane asylum for years (and, by all accounts, for good reason). It seems doubtful Otto was ever cognizant of the fact that he was king.

Acknowledgments

Grateful acknowledgment is made to the following publications in which these poems originally appeared:

Arden: "Driving at Dusk in Open Country," "The Novel of Grisly Details," "Valley of You" (in somewhat different form as "From a Line in Richard Wilbur's Prose")

Borderlands: Texas Poetry Review: "For the Drowned"

Center: "Outing"

Concho River Review: "Vermeer's Window"

Ekphrasis: "View of Delft with a Musical Instrument Dealer"

The Paris Review: "Lucky Strikes," "A Made-for-TV Movie," "My Work with the King" (as "My Work with Ludwig II"), "A Palace for the Heart," "Postcoital," "Song," "Stevens in a Swarm of Gnats"

Pleiades: "The Morning's News" (as "On the Death of Ludwig II and his Court-Appointed Psychiatrist"), "Pillbox"

The Red River Review: "After Midnight in the Mountains," "Hill-Climbing"

Southwest Review: "The Gardener's Tale"

The Texas Poetry Calendar 2002: "Bluebonnets" (in slightly different form)

The Wallace Stevens Journal: "Invective Against Swan Songs"

Western Humanities Review: "Burne-Jones, in the National Gallery, Views *The Arnolfini Marriage* One Last Time," "Dichotomies"

"For the Drowned" also appeared in *Texas in Poetry 2: An Anthology of Poetry about Texas*. TCU Press, 2002.

I would like to give special thanks to Richard Howard, whose continued encouragement, support, and direction have sustained me through the long gestation of this volume; to Andrew Hudgins, whose support and direction have proven invaluable to me in this endeavor and numerous others; and to Shawn Sturgeon, without whose friendship and support this book would not exist. I would also like to give thanks to a number of friends and mentors whose fellowship and passion for writing have been instrumental: Cicero Bruce, Scott Cairns, Ron Carlson, Dot Carmichael, Christina Davis, Mark Dodson, Elke Herbst, Jim Linebarger, Dianne Knight, Deneé Pescarmona, Clay Reynolds, Kay Sands, Grant Sisk, Michael Spence, Willard Spiegelman, Mark Strand, Bob Street, Wanda Strukus, and Suzi Rodgers Whaley. Thanks also, and always, to my family.